Sidney Crosby

By Kylie Burns

Crabtree Publishing Company

www.crabtreebooks.com

Crabtree Publishing Company

www.crabtreebooks.com

Author: Kylie Burns
Publishing plan research and development: Reagan Miller
Editors: Molly Aloian, Crystal Sikkens
Proofreader and indexer: Wendy Scavuzzo
Photo research: Crystal Sikkens
Designer: Ken Wright
Production coordinator and prepress technician: Ken Wright
Print coordinator: Margaret Amy Salter

Photographs:
Alamy: © ZUMA Press, Inc.: pages 9, 22, 23, 27; © Greg Fiume/NewSport/ZUMAPRESS. com: page 18
Associated Press: pages 5, 10, 14, 15, 16, 21, 26
Getty Images: NHLI via Getty Images: pages 6–7; Bruce Bennett/Staff: page 8; Dave Sandford/ Stringer: pages 11, 12–13; Gregory Shamus/ Stringer: page 17; Carlos Osorio/Toronto Star: page 19
Keystone Press: zumapress.com: pages 1, 4, 20, 24, 25, 28
Wikimedia: Michael Miller: cover

Every effort has been made to trace copyright holders and to obtain their permission for use of copyright material. The authors and publishers would be pleased to rectify any error or omission in future editions. All the Internet addresses given in this book were correct at the time of going to press. The author and publishers regret any inconvenience caused if addresses have changed or sites have ceased to exist, but can accept no responsibility for any such changes.

Library and Archives Canada Cataloguing in Publication

Burns, Kylie, author
    Sidney Crosby / Kylie Burns.

(Superstars!)
Includes index.
Issued in print and electronic formats.
ISBN 978-0-7787-0038-8 (bound).--ISBN 978-0-7787-0068-5 (pbk.).--ISBN 978-1-4271-9386-5 (pdf).--ISBN 978-1-4271-9380-3 (html)

    1. Crosby, Sidney, 1987- --Juvenile literature. 2. Hockey players--Canada--Biography--Juvenile literature. I. Title. II. Series: Superstars! (St. Catharines, Ont.)

GV848.5.C76B87 2013   j796.962092   C2013-905223-2
    C2013-905224-0

Library of Congress Cataloging-in-Publication Data

Burns, Kylie.
    Sidney Crosby / Kylie Burns.
       pages cm. -- (Superstars!)
    Includes index.
    ISBN 978-0-7787-0038-8 (reinforced library binding : alk. paper) --ISBN 978-0-7787-0068-5 (pbk. : alk. paper) -- ISBN 978-1-4271-9386-5 (electronic pdf : alk. paper) -- ISBN 978-1-4271-9380-3 (electronic html : alk. paper)
    1. Crosby, Sidney, 1987---Juvenile literature. 2. Hockey players--Canada--Biography--Juvenile literature. I. Title.

GV848.5.C76B87 2013
796.962092--dc23
[B]
    2013033216

Crabtree Publishing Company

www.crabtreebooks.com   1-800-387-7650

Printed in Canada/092013/BF20130815

Published in Canada
Crabtree Publishing
616 Welland Ave.
St. Catharines, ON

Published in the United States
Crabtree Publishing
PMB 59051
350 Fifth Avenue, 59th Floor
New York, New York 10118

Published in the United Kingdom
Crabtree Publishing
Maritime House
Basin Road North, Hove
BN41 1WR

Published in Australia
Crabtree Publishing
3 Charles Street
Coburg North
VIC 3058

CONTENTS

Shooting Star 4

A Star Is Born 6

Living the Dream 10

In the Zone...16

The Gold Standard..24

Timeline 29

Glossary 30

Find Out More..31

Index..32

Words that are defined in the glossary are in
bold type the first time they appear in the text.

Shooting Star

The Canadian centerman Sidney Crosby sizes up the ice, winding his way past the defence with speed and skill. It's sudden-death overtime in the final hockey game of the Canada-versus-United States match-up in the 2010 Winter Olympics. The score is 2–2, and Sidney is feeling the pressure to score. "Sid the Kid" chases the puck in the corner and makes a perfect pass to teammate Jerome Iginla, who quickly passes it right back to Sidney in front of the net. The Canadian fans are on their feet, breathless and hopeful…will this be it? Will this be the goal to win Olympic Gold?

Fire on the Ice

For many athletes, this kind of pressure can have a negative effect on their performance. Sidney Crosby uses that pressure to push himself emotionally and physically on the ice. With over 40 awards, trophies, and medals to his name, Sidney Crosby is one of the best Canadian hockey players of all time. It's all in a day's work for this superstar hockey player!

Sidney Crosby is often called "The Next One" because he reminds people of "The Great One," hockey hero Wayne Gretzky.

All Star

Since he was **drafted** in 2005 by the National Hockey League's Pittsburgh Penguins, Sidney has earned many titles, including Most Valuable Player and Most Outstanding Player. He was also the youngest player to be chosen for the First All-Star Team. Sidney Crosby's dream to play in the NHL has come true, and he has achieved even more than that in a short time. He is one of the world's most loved sports figures.

FAN FAVORITE

Growing up watching hockey, Sidney Crosby's favorite player was Steve Yzerman. Now Yzerman is a fan of Sidney Crosby!

Sidney's hockey hero Steve Yzerman celebrates a Stanley Cup victory with the Detroit Red Wings in 1997.

He Said It

"He's a great example for all young players that here we have one of the best players in our game, a young guy just driven to get better in all areas."
—Steve Yzerman, commenting on Sidney Crosby in an article in *The Canadian Press*, Dec. 2010

A Star Is Born

Sidney Patrick Crosby was born in Cole Harbour, Nova Scotia, on August 7, 1987. As a child, he spent hours shooting pucks in his basement. Today, he has one of the best shots in the league. Sidney's parents, Troy and Trina Crosby, knew that their son had talent at a very young age. Sidney was passing the puck and scoring goals earlier than most of his **peers**. His impressive skills on the ice were the subject of a local newspaper story when he was only seven years old! By the age of 17, he was the NHL's number-one draft pick.

WHAT'S IN A NUMBER?

Sidney wears the number 87 on his jersey. He picked the number because it had a special meaning: "8" is the month he was born (August), and "7" is the day, in the year 1987!

Take Your Best Shot

Sidney's first practice rink wasn't a rink at all—it was the basement of his family's home. He took shots on the clothes dryer with pucks and rubber balls because he didn't have a hockey net. Aiming for the small opening in the dryer forced Sidney to have a very precise shot. He practiced every day, and put a lot of dents in the dryer. The only time Sidney couldn't practice on the dryer was when his laundry was being dried!

Overcoming Obstacles

When Sidney began playing competitive ice hockey, it became difficult for his family to pay for equipment and travel expenses. Instead of giving up on hockey, Sidney's mom Trina took a second job. With the extra money she earned, Sidney's parents could afford to provide their son with the opportunities that helped shape him into the star player he is today.

Sidney comes from a close-knit family. He is pictured here with his younger sister Taylor, mom Trina, and dad Troy.

Like Father, Like Son

Sidney was born into a hockey family. His dad Troy was drafted by the Montreal Canadiens in the 1984 Entry Draft. He was a goalie, but he never actually played a game for the Canadiens. Sidney looked up to his dad. He wanted to learn all he could about the game of hockey so he could be drafted one day, too.

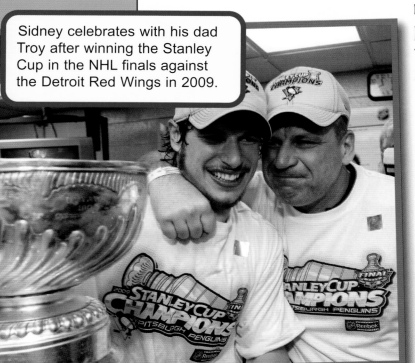

Sidney celebrates with his dad Troy after winning the Stanley Cup in the NHL finals against the Detroit Red Wings in 2009.

Sid the Kid

When he was young, Sidney was denied opportunities to play for teams that were older than his age group, despite his skills. The Cole Harbour Hockey Association rejected his parents' request to allow their 12-year-old son to play on a team with 15-year-olds. At only 5'2" (157 cm) and weighing 110 pounds (50 kg), Sidney was considered too small to play full-contact against NHL-sized 15-year-olds. The coach broke the rules and put him in the game anyway. Sidney scored a goal and three assists, helping his team win. The coach received a one-game **suspension**, but Sidney was banned from playing for older-age teams.

Making the Grade

Sidney was an excellent student. He maintained straight A's even though he often missed school to play hockey. Sidney went to Astral Drive Junior High School until he was 15. He moved to Minnesota to play for the Shattuck-Saint Mary's Boarding School hockey team. He led the team to a National AAA Championship in 2003. Sidney then moved to Moncton, New Brunswick, to play for the Rimouski Oceanic Junior team in the Quebec Major Junior Hockey League. He attended Harrison Trimble High School in Moncton, graduating in 2005.

Like Brother, Like Sister

Taylor Crosby is nine years younger than her big brother Sidney. They never went to the same school together, but Taylor has followed in her brother's footsteps and attends Shattuck-Saint Mary's school in Minnesota. Like her brother, Taylor is also a hockey player, but she is a goalie.

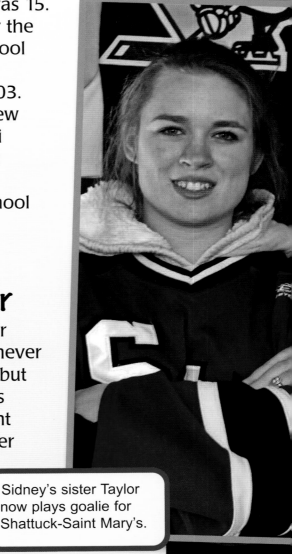

Sidney's sister Taylor now plays goalie for Shattuck-Saint Mary's.

She Said It

"*I know I'm my own person. I try to use him as a role model and (follow) his work ethic, but I don't compare myself to him. I'm never going to be him and he's never going to be me.*"
—Taylor Crosby, *The Globe and Mail*, June 7, 2013

9

Living the Dream

Sidney Crosby was drafted as the first overall pick in the 2003 Midget Draft to play for the Rimouski Oceanic team in the QMJHL. He quickly won the attention of Canadian Junior Hockey fans with his scoring skills. At just 15 years old, he became the first player to win all of the league's top awards: Top Rookie, Top Scorer, and Most Valuable Player.

Silver Streak

Sidney's incredible skills and leadership led to the opportunity of a lifetime—the invitation to play for Canada in the 2004 World Junior Championship. Sidney was the youngest player on the team at age 16. Team Canada came away with the silver medal.

Rimouski Oceanic's Sidney Crosby heads back onto the ice during a game against the Quebec Remparts on December 5, 2003.

Sweet Dreams

Playing for Team Canada was a dream come true for Sidney Crosby. But a silver medal was not enough for him—he wanted to go for gold! The chance came the following year in 2005 when Sidney joined Team Canada at the World Junior Championships in Grand Forks, North Dakota. Team Canada was stacked with a lot of talented players, but a strong Russian Junior Team was determined to shut down the Canadian powerhouse to claim the gold medal for themselves.

Sidney Crosby said winning the World Junior Championships was a dream come true and something he would share with his teammates forever.

Power Play

That year, the NHL experienced a **lockout** which canceled the 2004–2005 season. The World Junior Championships was the first televised hockey that fans had seen in months. The pressure was on, and Sidney Crosby and his team didn't disappoint. They won the gold medal, beating the Russians 6–1 in the final.

11

A Win and a Loss

After celebrating the big win at the World Juniors, Sidney returned home to Quebec to resume his place with the Rimouski Oceanic Team. When he unpacked his suitcase, he got a shock—his hockey jersey from the tournament had gone missing! It had great **sentimental value** to Sidney and he was very upset that it was gone. Newspapers ran the story and all of Canada was on alert for the missing red jersey.

Too Much Baggage

A few days after the jersey went missing, it turned up in Gatineau, Quebec. The thief had placed it in a plastic bag and dropped it in a mailbox! A baggage handler at the airport in Montreal had stolen the sweater from Sidney's bag. He was charged with theft and had to pay a fine of $5000.

Lost and Found

Hockey players travel constantly, so equipment often goes missing. Sidney has lost many items over the years in addition to his World Junior Championship jersey. Some of those include a jersey Sidney wore in his first NHL game, a glove, and the hockey stick he used to score in the 2010 Olympics "golden goal." Luckily for Sidney Crosby, every missing item found its way back to him!

The Shirt off His Back

Hockey players often donate their hockey equipment to charities. The charities then sell the items at **auctions** to raise money. Sidney Crosby's jerseys have sold for between $21,000 and $47,000 at auctions. The jersey he wore in his third game in the NHL sold for $21,010 in support of those affected by the devastation of Hurricane Katrina in 2005.

When he played for Team Canada, Sidney Crosby wore the number 9.

Winning the Lottery

In 2005, the **NHL Draft Lottery** was given a special nickname: the "Sidney Crosby Sweepstakes." The Pittsburgh Penguins won the lottery, giving them first choice of the draft picks. They quickly snapped up the promising young superstar. To this day, Sidney Crosby has never played for another NHL team.

PART OF THE FAMILY

Hockey legend Mario Lemieux was the captain and part-owner of the Pittsburgh Penguins when Sidney Crosby was drafted. Sidney lived with Lemieux's family for the first five years of his career.

Mario Lemieux looks on as Sidney Crosby signs his first NHL contract on September 9th, 2005.

He Said It

"I've won the Stanley Cup, won gold medals. Getting Sidney Crosby was the happiest day of my life."
—Penguins' executive Craig Patrick, in an article by Eric Adelson for *ESPN magazine*, 2006

Late Night Television

Soon after the Penguins signed Sidney, television shows wanted interviews with the newly-drafted star. A week after the draft picks, Sidney appeared on the *Tonight Show* with Jay Leno. Sidney and Jay Leno shot pucks into a dryer, just like Sidney did as a kid.

Sidney's television appearances include several talk shows as well as commercials for Reebok, Dempster's Bread, and Gatorade. He also appeared in a movie called *She's Out of My League*.

Face-off

When Sidney Crosby was drafted to the Pittsburgh Penguins, another young player was starting his NHL career with the Washington Capitals. Russian hockey star Alexander Ovechkin was the number-one draft pick one year before Crosby. Because of the NHL lockout in 2004, however, Ovechkin and Crosby started playing in the same season— 2005–2006. Crosby's style of play is hard-working and **humble**, but Ovechkin celebrates every goal in a big, showy way. They compete for many of the same trophies and awards, and their point totals are often similar.

In the Zone

By 2005, Sidney Crosby was becoming a household name. Along with his new fame, Sidney was dealing with a rigorous practice schedule and **rivalries** with other hockey players. Despite these challenges, Sidney remained focused on his goals and continued to play the best hockey he could.

Rivals Ovechkin and Crosby became teammates in 2006 when they were both named to the First All-Star Team, a team made up of the best players in the NHL.

Taking the Hits

Sidney is no stranger to rivalry and negativity—it began early in his minor hockey career in Nova Scotia. He was often targeted in games by opposing players who wanted him off the ice. Other players' parents also treated him with insults and threats, hoping to throw him off his game so their own kids could shine. It was so bad that he chose not to wear his hockey jersey between games at tournaments so he wouldn't be recognized!

Point Streak

Sidney Crosby didn't let negative attention get him down. In fact, it fueled his desire to be better, stronger, and faster. Now 5'11" (180 cm) and 200 pounds (91 kg), he's not the biggest player in the NHL. But some say what he lacks in size, he makes up for in effort. When he made his NHL debut against the New Jersey Devils on October 5, 2005, he assisted a goal by teammate Mark Recchi, earning him his first point in the NHL.

First Goal

Crosby's first NHL goal came three days after his first assist. He was playing a home game at Mellon Arena in Pittsburgh against the Boston Bruins. With his parents watching in the stands, Crosby edged the puck past the goalie, Hannu Toivonen, then celebrated his first goal with his fellow teammates. Despite losing the game 7−6 in overtime that night, all of Pittsburgh seemed to cheer for the young **rookie** who was breathing new life into the team.

Sidney kept the puck as a souvenir of his first NHL goal. He wrapped it in tape and wrote across it: "1st NHL goal, October 8th, 2005."

17

The Winds of Change

During Sidney's first year on the team, many changes took place. Team management decided to hire a new coach. Michel Therrien made Sidney an alternate captain of the Pittsburgh Penguins. He was formerly head coach of the Montreal Canadiens—Sidney's favorite team as a boy. The day after he was hired, Therrien made Sidney an alternate, or assistant, captain of the Penguins. Many people didn't agree with this choice, but Therrien and current team captain Mario Lemieux were confident Sidney could handle the responsibility.

No Captain

In January 2006, because of heart problems, Sidney's good friend and captain Mario Lemieux announced he was retiring early from hockey. This left the Penguins without a captain for the 2006–2007 season. Sidney was one of four alternate captains that led the team that year.

Crosby is seen here (left) skating beside fellow alternate captain Mark Recchi.

Top of the Pile

The 2006–2007 NHL season proved to be a turnaround year for Sidney Crosby. He led the team to a spot in the NHL playoffs. Sidney had dreamed of winning the Stanley Cup someday, and the Penguins' successful season gave him hope, spurring him on to play even harder. He had 36 goals in 79 games, making him the top scoring player in the NHL at just 19 years old.

An Upset

Going into the Eastern Conference quarterfinals, Sidney had a newfound hunger for the ultimate goal: the Stanley Cup. Sidney fought hard, earning five points in five games but, in the end, his team lost the series. Sidney's hope of fulfilling that dream had to wait.

Sidney Crosby poses with the Lester B. Pearson, Hart, and Art Ross Memorial Trophies that he won at the NHL Awards in Toronto on June 14, 2007.

Lead the Way

At the end of the 2006–2007 season, the Penguins knew they needed an inspiring captain to lead the team. Sidney had been offered the captain position during the season, but turned it down. However, on May 31, 2007, Sidney was ready to accept the responsibility and was named team captain, making him the youngest captain in NHL history.

A New Season

In 2007–2008, Sidney scored 24 goals and 48 assists in his first season as captain. He helped his team finish in second place as Atlantic Division Champions in the Eastern Conference with 102 points. He led his team into the playoffs once again.

After May 31, 2007, the letter "A," standing for alternate captain, on Sidney's jersey was replaced with "C" for captain.

He Said It

"... I was not ready to accept that responsibility quite yet. Going through the playoffs and having that experience has probably given me more confidence. I understand there is going to be a lot more responsibility on my shoulders with this, but it's something I'm ready for..."

–On becoming captain in *The Record*, June 1, 2007

Neighbors, Not Friends

In 2008, during the Eastern Conference Finals, Sidney's Penguins played against the Flyers. After winning Game 5, the Penguins were the Conference champions and were moving on for a shot at the Stanley Cup.

Seeing Red

In the final round of the Stanley Cup Championship, the Penguins were up against the Western Conference champions, the Detroit Red Wings. The Penguins were down 3 games to 2 heading into Game 6. Unfortunately, the Penguins' quest for the cup ended there when the team lost to the Red Wings 3–2.

BAD LUCK

When the Penguins won the Eastern Conference Final, Sidney refused to **hoist** the trophy and carry it around the ice. Most team captains won't hold any trophy other than the Stanley Cup because they think it will bring the team bad luck!

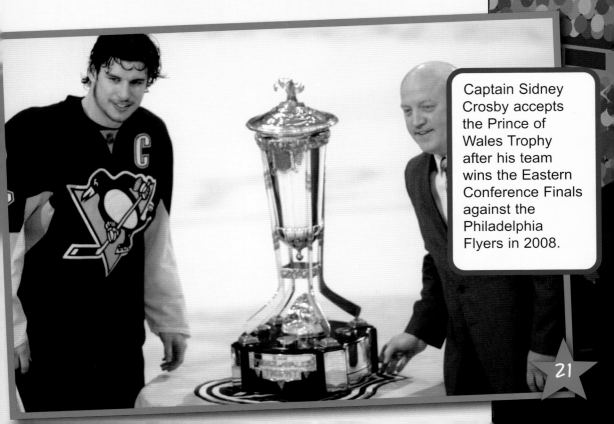

Captain Sidney Crosby accepts the Prince of Wales Trophy after his team wins the Eastern Conference Finals against the Philadelphia Flyers in 2008.

The Offensive Zone

After the difficult loss in the finals of the 2007–2008 Stanley Cup Playoffs, Sidney Crosby came back stronger the following season. He achieved several **milestones** in the 2008–2009 regular season. His career totals soared to more than 100 goals, 200 assists, and 300 points overall!

Collision

The Penguins got another chance to take on the Red Wings for the Stanley Cup as the two teams advanced to the final round of the 2009 Stanley Cup Championship. With the series tied at three games a piece, the Stanley Cup Champions will be decided in Game 7. In the second period of the final game, Sidney took a clean hit from Detroit Red Wings' Johan Franzen that injured his knee. He hobbled off the ice as his teammates watched their captain leave the most important game of his NHL career.

Pain registers on Sidney Crosby's face as he receives a hard check from Red Wings' Johan Franzen during the seventh game of the Stanley Cup Final in 2009.

Sidney, Meet...Stanley!

Not one to abandon his team, Sidney tried to return in the third period but he only skated 32 seconds before heading back to the bench. With just six minutes, seven seconds left in the game, Detroit's Jonathon Ericsson narrowed the gap with a goal, making it 2–1. Sidney watched as his team fought hard to keep the lead. When the buzzer finally sounded, Sidney's team had outplayed Detroit to become the new Stanley Cup Champions!

Crosby hoists the Stanley Cup after achieving the ultimate goal of his career– Stanley Cup Champion on June 12, 2009.

The Ultimate Prize

Sidney hobbled back onto the ice for a victory lap. It wasn't exactly how he had pictured it, but Sidney Crosby finally achieved his goal of winning the Stanley Cup. He was the youngest captain to win the cup and he earned it! In 24 playoff games, Sidney had scored the most goals of any player with a total of 15.

23

The Gold Standard

As a child, Sidney had a dream to represent his country as an Olympic athlete. He was denied the chance at the 2006 Winter Olympics. At the age of 19, he was considered too young and inexperienced for international hockey. Four years later, he got the call he had been waiting for. He was asked to represent Canada at the 2010 Winter Olympics in Vancouver. He was going to play for his country at the Olympics in a Canadian city. It was a no-brainer. He immediately accepted the offer.

Sidney was named alternate captain for the 2010 Canadian Olympic hockey team.

Sudden-Death

Sidney played well throughout the Olympics, scoring 7 points in 7 games. Two teams made it to the final game: Canada and the United States—long-time rivals and fierce competitors. By the end of regulation time, they were tied at 2–2. Then the third period buzzer rang out. It was sudden-death overtime, and the pressure was on. Crosby and his team gave it everything they had.

Pure Gold

In a moment of glory, Sidney scored the game-winning overtime goal against the United States in the gold-medal Olympic championship game. The whole nation celebrated Sidney's "golden goal." Sidney Crosby was a Canadian hockey hero!

Team Canada's Sidney Crosby scored the "golden goal" in overtime against the United States at the 2010 Olympics, earning Canada the gold medal.

No Pain, No Gain

Being an athlete has a downside. Injuries are common in professional sports. Sidney suffered two significant hits to the head in two back-to-back games in 2011, resulting in **concussion** symptoms such as dizziness and headaches. His injuries forced him to miss the rest of the regular season as well as the Stanley Cup Playoffs that year. However, the incredible athlete still managed to be the top-scoring player for the Penguins, earning 66 points in just 41 games. No other Pittsburgh Penguin had ever earned that many points in so few games. Sidney was injured, and still managed to set new records!

Toothless Wonder

On March 30, 2013, Sidney experienced a broken jaw and lost several teeth when he was hit in the face with a puck during a game against the New York Islanders. His teammate Brooks Orpik took a slap shot that **deflected** and struck Sidney below his visor, sending teeth flying out of his mouth along with his mouth guard. Sidney said he never saw the shot coming.

When Crosby returned to the ice, he was careful to protect his face with a metal cage below his visor.

A Heart of Gold

Sidney Crosby did not grow up in a wealthy home. He is now very rich, and he understands that fame and fortune can be used to help others. He generously participates in many charity opportunities to lend a hand to those in need. In 2008, he partnered with the Make A Wish Foundation to bring children living with cancer to an NHL game with their friends and family.

Giving Back

The following year, he started the Sidney Crosby Foundation to help children and children's charities. His foundation teamed up with the National Hockey League Players' Association (NHLPA) in 2011 to provide children from his home province of Nova Scotia with hockey equipment that would outfit 87 different teams among the Minor Hockey Programs. The donation was worth more than $40,000 and brought joy to many young Canadian hockey players on 10 different teams.

Children's charities are important to Sidney. Here, he is pictured with some of his Pittsburgh Penguins teammates during a team visit to a children's hospital.

Sign on the Dotted Line

Sidney Crosby has received offers from companies such as Bell, Reebok, Tim Hortons, and Gatorade to **endorse** their products. Companies know that people want to buy what champions wear, eat, and use. Reebok, a sportswear manufacturer, signed Sidney Crosby to a multi-million dollar deal to become a spokesperson for the company when Sidney was only 18 years old. In 2010, he signed a new deal with Reebok for 1.4 million dollars per season over five to seven years, making this the biggest endorsement deal in the NHL's history. In addition to endorsing hockey equipment, Sidney promotes his line of sportswear called SC87, which is also manufactured by Reebok.

Sidney regularly takes time to sign autographs for fans. Here, a young fan proudly hands Sidney a drawing he made of the famous hockey player.

Power Play

Sidney Crosby is not just a hockey player; he is a superstar. He signed an extended contract with the Penguins for $104.4 million until the year 2025. He manages to find time to play a sport he loves, gets paid an enormous amount of money to do it, and then gives back to his community in charitable ways. He is a captain, an Olympian, a spokesperson, a role model, and the head of the Sidney Crosby Foundation. Amazingly, it all started with a little boy's love of hockey and a big dream.

Timeline

1987: Born August 7 in Cole Harbour, Nova Scotia, Canada

1994: Featured on a National Television program at the age of 7

2002: Moves away from home to attend Shattuck-Saint Mary's school in the United States

2003: The QMJHL drafts Crosby to the Rimouski Oceanic Team

2003: Plays for the Canadian Junior Hockey Team, winning the Gold Medal

2005: Graduated from Harrison Trimble High School in Moncton, New Brunswick

2005: The NHL Draft number-one pick, Sidney Crosby, is drafted by the Pittsburgh Penguins

2007: Named captain of the Penguins, becoming the youngest captain in NHL history

2007: Named one of *TIME* Magazine's Top 100 Most Influential People

2007: Designs a clothing line called SC87

2008: First time in the playoffs for the Stanley Cup

2008: Achieved his 100th goal, 200th assist, and 300th point

2009: Wins the Stanley Cup for the first time, becoming the youngest captain to do so

2010: Scores the "golden goal" at the Olympic Games in overtime giving Canada the gold medal

2011: Suffers two hits resulting in a concussion, misses last 42 games of the season and the Stanley Cup playoffs

2012: Signs a contract extension worth $104.4 million through the 2024–2025 season with the Penguins

2013: Suffers a broken jaw from a teammate's slap shot

2013: Makes it to the semi-finals of the Stanley Cup playoffs, losing to the Boston Bruins

Glossary

auctions Sales at which people bid on items they wish to buy

concussion An injury to the brain caused by a hard blow or collision

deflected Turned or caused to turn aside from a specific direction

drafted Chosen by a team to be one of its players

endorse To say that a product or service is good or effective and to encourage others to try it

hoist To lift over one's head

humble Modest; not proud or bold

lockout A period of time when the NHL and the Players' Association do not have an agreement and the owners lock out the players

milestones Important points in one's development or progress

NHL Draft Lottery The yearly event in which a non-playoff team is chosen by a random draw to have the first choice selection of eligible players in the NHL draft

peers People of the same rank or class

penalty Punishment for breaking the rules in play—it results in a player sitting out for a set period of time

rivalries Competitions between one or more people or groups for the same prize or goal

rookie A brand new player in his or her first year of a professional sport

sentimental value When something is important to someone because of the feelings or memories associated with it

suspension A period of time in which a player or coach may not participate in a sport as a result of behaving inappropriately

Find Out More

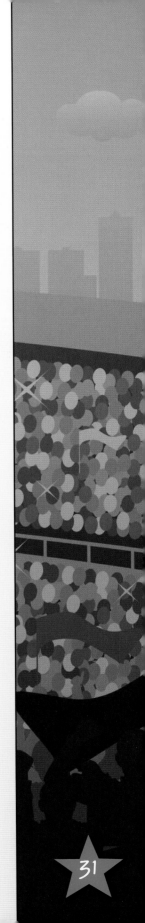

Books

Joyce, Gare. *Sidney Crosby: Taking the Game by Storm*. Markham, ON: Fitzhenry & Whiteside, 2007.

Hollingsworth, Paul. *Sidney Crosby: The Story of a Champion*. Halifax, NS: Nimbus Publishing, 2010.

Leclair, Danielle. *Sidney Crosby* (My Life). Calgary, AB: Weigl Educational Publishers Limited, 2011.

Poulton, J. Alexander. *Sidney Crosby*. Montreal, QC: OverTime Books, 2008.

Websites

The National Hockey League Players Association (NHLPA)
www.nhlpa.com/news/sidney-crosby-and-goals-dreams-help-more-children-play-hockey
Information about Sidney's charitable causes

The Internet Hockey Database
www.hockeydb.com
For all the stats on Sid the Kid!

The Pittsburgh Penguins official site
http://penguins.nhl.com
Learn more about Sidney Crosby and his teammates

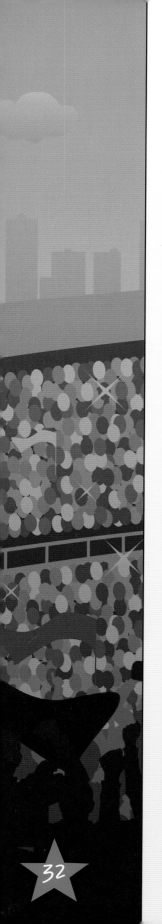

Index

alternate captain, 18
awards, 4, 5, 10
captain, 20, 24
championships, 9, 10, 20
charities, 13, 27, 28
childhood, 6
clothes dryer, 7, 15
Cole Harbour Hockey
   Association, 8
commercials, 15
contracts, 14, 28, 29
Crosby, Taylor, 9
Crosby, Troy, 8
Detroit Red Wings, 8, 21,
   22-23
draft picks, 4, 6, 10, 14-15
Eastern Conference Finals,
   21
education, 9
endorsements, 15, 28
family, 7, 9
fans, 28
First All-Star Team, 16
first NHL goal, 17
injuries, 22-23, 26
jerseys, 6, 12, 13, 20
Lemieux, Mario, 14, 18
lockout, 11, 15
lost equipment, 12-13
medals, 4, 10, 11, 25
Montreal Canadiens, 8

obstacles, 7, 8, 16
Olympics, 4, 24-25
Ovechkin, Alexander, 15, 16
penalties, 18
Pittsburgh Penguins, 5, 14,
   17-23
playoffs, 19, 20, 22, 26
points, 19, 20, 22
Quebec Major Junior Hockey
   League (QMJHL), 9, 10
Recchi, Mark, 17, 18
Rimouski Oceanic, 9, 10, 12
rivalries, 16
SC87 sportswear line, 28
Shattuck-Saint Mary's
   Boarding School, 9
She's Out of My League, 15
shooting pucks, 7
"Sid the Kid," 4
Sidney Crosby Foundation,
   27
Stanley Cup, 19, 21, 22, 23
Team Canada, 11, 13, 24-25
"The Next One," 4
Therrien, Michel, 18
Tonight Show, 15
trophies, 4, 19, 21
World Junior
   Championships, 10, 11
Yzerman, Steve, 5

About the Author

Kylie Burns is a part-time freelance writer and a full-time teacher. She has written children's books on a variety of cool topics, including science, sports, character education, math, and history. She feels grateful to teach children all day—then write for them at night! At home, she has three great kids, a supportive husband, and one very demanding guinea pig.